Our world

Our families

from baby to grandma

Monica Hughes

Little Nippers

www.heinemann.co.uk/library
Visit our website to find out more information about **Heinemann Library** books.

To order:
☎ Phone 44 (0) 1865 888066
📄 Send a fax to 44 (0) 1865 314091
💻 Visit the Heinemann Bookshop at www.heinemann.co.uk/library to browse our catalogue and order online.

First published in Great Britain by Heinemann Library, Halley Court, Jordan Hill, Oxford OX2 8EJ, part of Harcourt Education. Heinemann is a registered trademark of Harcourt Education Ltd.

Editorial: Jilly Attwood and Claire Throp
Design: Jo Hinton-Malivoire and bigtop, Bicester, UK
Models made by: Jo Brooker
Picture Research: Catherine Bevan
Production: Lorraine Warner

Originated by Dot Gradations
Printed and bound in China by South China Printing Company

ISBN 0 431 16253 0 (hardback)
06 05 04 03 02
10 9 8 7 6 5 4 3 2 1

ISBN 0 431 16258 1 (paperback)
06 05 04 03 02
10 9 8 7 6 5 4 3 2 1

British Library Cataloguing in Publication Data
Hughes, Monica
Our families
306.8'5
A full catalogue record for this book is available from the British Library.

Acknowledgements
The publishers would like to thank the following for permission to reproduce photographs:
All photographs by Tudor Photography.

Cover photograph reproduced with permission of Tudor Photography.

The publishers would like to thank Annie Davy for her assistance in the preparation of this book.

Every effort has been made to contact copyright holders of any material reproduced in this book. Any omissions will be rectified in subsequent printings if notice is given to the publishers.

Contents

Tiffany and her family

Hello! I'm Tiffany and this is my family.

Jordan and his family

I'm Jordan and this is my family.

Who is in your family?

5

Sam and his family

Hello! I'm Sam and this is my family.

Louisa and her family

I'm Louisa and this is my family.

Mum

My Mum brushes my hair.

My Mum lets me help
her wash the car.

Scrub!

Scrub!

What do you do
with your Mum?

Dad

My Dad makes lovely meals.

Yum!

My Daddy reads to me at bedtime.

Who reads to you?

Brothers

My baby brother
makes a lot of noise.

My brother sleeps
on the top bunk.

Do you have
a brother?

Sisters

My big sister lets me try on her make up.

Do you have a sister?

15

Grandpa

My Grandpa Slater helps me to ride my bike.

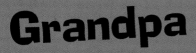

My Grandad died when I was tiny.

I like looking at pictures of him.

17

Granny

My Granny has got wrinkly skin.

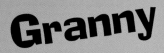

My Grandma takes me to feed the ducks.

What do you do with your Granny?

19

My aunty lets me use her computer.

My uncle is my Dad's brother.
He plays football with us.

Cousins

It's fun when my cousins come to play.

My Grandpa Slater is
their grandpa too.

My cousin is only a baby.

Do you have cousins?

Index

The end

Notes for adults

This series supports the child's knowledge and understanding of their world, in particular their personal, social and emotional development area. The following Early Learning Goals are relevant to the series:
• respond to significant experiences, showing a range of feelings when appropriate
• have a developing awareness of their own needs, views and feelings and be sensitive to the needs and feelings of others
• have a developing respect for their own cultures and beliefs and those of other people.

This book introduces different families and it is important that the child feels that their own family is 'special' regardless of how many members it has and whatever the relationships. **Our Families** provides plenty of opportunity for the child to compare and contrast their own experiences with those of the children depicted in the book. This can be encouraged by asking open-ended questions like: Who is in your family? How is your family like this family? Do you have family that you see only on special occasions? There is also the opportunity to talk about family members who have died, but this will need to be introduced with sensitivity. The concept of second families or step-families can also be touched upon.

The series will help the child extend their vocabulary. Some words related to **Our Families** could include *parent, adult, older* and *younger, nephew, niece, grandson/daughter, relation* and *generation*.

Follow-up activities
The child could collect (or draw) pictures of their family and make a family tree or their very own **Our Families** book. They could use the home corner to role-play different family activities.